Ice Hockey

Ice Hockey

Mike Kennedy

Watts LIBRARY™

Franklin Watts
A Division of Scholastic Inc.
New York • Toronto • London • Auckland • Sydney
Mexico City • New Delhi • Hong Kong
Danbury, Connecticut

Note to readers: Definitions for words in **bold** can be found in the Glossary at the back of this book.

Photographs © 2003: AllSport USA/Getty Images/Robert Laberge: 36; AP/Wide World Photos: 17, 27 (Kevork Djansezian), 18 (Jim Rogash), 43 (Steven Senne), 5 left, 20, 42 (Andrew Vaughan), 26 (Adrian Wyld), 15 (David Zalubowski), 14 top, 49, 52; Bruce Bennett Studios: 40 (M. Digiacomo), 6 (J. Giamundo), 53 (Wen Roberts), 10, 14 bottom, 31; Corbis Images/Reuters NewMedia Inc.: 47; Getty Images: 44 (Scott Cunningham), 23 (Scott Cunningham/NHLI), 32 (Robert Laberge); Hockey Hall of Fame: 12, 19; Shelly Castellano/SCPIX.com: cover, 2, 25; SportsChrome USA: 38 (Scott Brinegar), 28 (Brian Drake), 34 (C. Melvin), 22 (Rob Tringali Jr.); Team Stewart, Inc./Illustrated Post Card Co., Montreal: 11; The Public Archives of Canada: 5 right, 9.

The photograph opposite the title page shows Wayne Gretzky, the top scorer in NHL history.

Library of Congress Cataloging-in-Publication Data

Kennedy, Mike (Mike William), 1965–
    Ice hockey / Mike Kennedy.
      p. cm.—(Watts library)
    Summary: Reviews the history of ice hockey, how it is played, the rules of the game, and introduces readers to some of hockey's greatest players.
    Includes bibliographical references and index.
    ISBN 0-531-12273-5 (lib. bdg.)   0-531-15590-0 (pbk.)
    1. Hockey—History—Juvenile literature. [1. Hockey.] I. Title. II. Series.
GV847.25 .K46 2003
796.962—dc21

2002015340

Contents

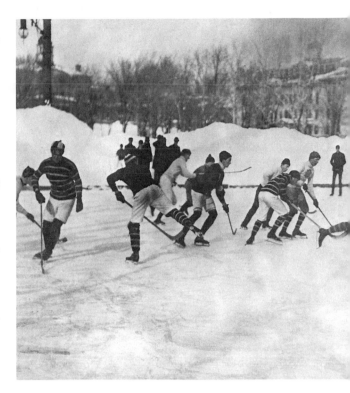

Ice hockey has evolved into a sport played and enjoyed by people of all ages.

Chapter One

Out of the Wilderness

Pinpointing the birthplace of ice hockey is difficult. A game called *kolven* was played in Holland in the 1600s, while in North America the Iroquois developed a hockey-like sport, which they enjoyed on frozen ponds in the St. Lawrence River Valley.

There is no doubt, however, that ice hockey found its most **ardent** supporters in Canada. British soldiers stationed along the frontier in the early 1800s played a game similar to hockey to

7

relieve the boredom of the long winters. Ice hockey evolved from there, and became the sport of choice among Canadian pioneers. Eventually they shared the game with others, and it spread throughout North America.

Lord Stanley's Cup

Early forms of ice hockey barely resembled the game played today in the National Hockey League (NHL). Rules varied from one region of Canada to another. Games were played outdoors on frozen ponds and rivers with as many as thirty skaters on each side. Forward passing was not allowed. Goalies were prohibited from dropping to the ice. Games lasted for hours, and play was interrupted only when the puck scooted into a snow bank or fell through a hole in the ice.

In the mid-1800s, players fashioned sticks from tree branches, and anything from a rubber ball to a pinecone to a tin can served as the puck. For protection, some players strapped thick mail-order catalogs to their legs. Goalies often used chest protectors made for baseball catchers.

In 1881 students at McGill University in Toronto wrote a new set of rules for ice hockey. The most notable rule limited

Ramblin' Man

In 1885 the number of players per side was reduced from nine to seven. Each team's lineup included a rover, whose job was to offer support on offense and defense. If the forwards launched an offensive attack, he jumped into the play. If an opponent gained control of the puck, he hurried back on defense.

This photo depicts an ice hockey game at McGill University in 1904.

each side to nine players. With fewer players, the ice was open for the best skaters and shooters to show off their skills. Fans loved this version of the sport. Four years later the first organized league formed in Kingston, Ontario.

With ice hockey's popularity growing, Frederick Arthur, otherwise known as Lord Stanley of Preston, offered a prize in 1892 for Canada's best amateur team. The competition for the Stanley Cup electrified the entire country. Any squad could challenge the current champion for the silver trophy. This helped focus the spotlight on ice hockey's first generation of stars, which included goalie Whitey Merritt, forward Dan Bain, defenseman Mike Grant, and rover Russell Bowie.

The Montreal Amateur Athletic Association team, known as the AAAs, captured the first Stanley Cup in 1893.

Going Pro

By the turn of the century, ice hockey had begun to develop a loyal following in the United States, particularly in the Midwest and Northeast. In 1904 a Michigan dentist named John "Doc" Gibson started the International Pro Hockey League, the first to pay all of its players. Soon indoor rinks able to host thousands of fans were constructed, and other professional circuits sprouted all over North America. The National Hockey Association (NHA) in eastern Canada and the Pacific Coast Hockey Association (PCHA) in the west were the most popular of the new leagues.

The NHA reduced teams to six players per side, and changed from two 30-minute periods to three 20-minute periods. In the PCHA, goalies were allowed to make kick saves and to sprawl on the ice. Players wore numbers on their jerseys. Teams kept detailed statistics, which fans could track in the sports pages. Ice hockey was beginning to look the way it does today.

The NHA and PCHA often butted heads, especially when it came to the Stanley Cup. Teams from each league regularly challenged one another for the trophy, and this rivalry benefited the pro game immensely. Fred "Cyclone" Taylor, "Phantom" Joe Malone, and Newsy Lalonde headlined a new wave

Montreal's Victoria Rink, pictured here, was one of ice hockey's first great indoor arenas.

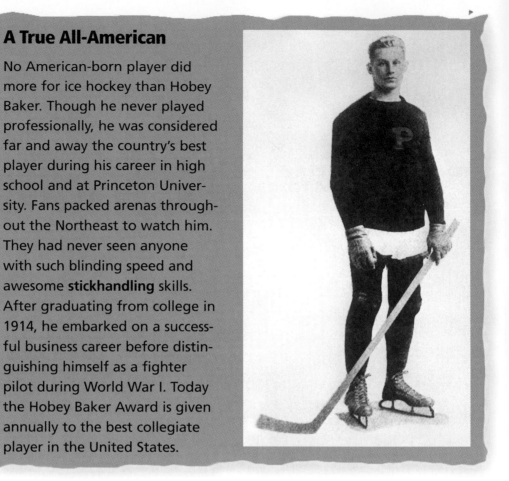

A True All-American

No American-born player did more for ice hockey than Hobey Baker. Though he never played professionally, he was considered far and away the country's best player during his career in high school and at Princeton University. Fans packed arenas throughout the Northeast to watch him. They had never seen anyone with such blinding speed and awesome **stickhandling** skills. After graduating from college in 1914, he embarked on a successful business career before distinguishing himself as a fighter pilot during World War I. Today the Hobey Baker Award is given annually to the best collegiate player in the United States.

of high-scoring stars, while Georges Vezina and Clint Benedict were kings of the **goal crease**.

Professional ice hockey suffered when World War I (1914–1918) broke out. Some of the sport's best players were called into military service, as were many fans. The NHA, **teetering** on the brink of bankruptcy, reorganized into the National Hockey League before the 1917–1918 season.

Although the NHL struggled initially, the league began to pick up momentum when the Montreal Canadiens and

Ottawa Senators developed into powerhouses. Their success attracted new fans and contributed to the **demise** of other pro circuits, including the PCHA. During the 1920s, the NHL established teams in major American cities like New York, Chicago, Detroit, and Boston, and the popularity of ice hockey grew even more.

Gold Standard

After surviving hard times during the Depression of the 1930s, the NHL entered what historians refer to as its Golden Age. The league had only six teams, so every squad featured a roster of All-Star caliber players. Maurice "Rocket" Richard, Max Bentley, Ted Lindsay, Teeder Kennedy, Bill Durnan, and Turk Broda all embarked on Hall of Fame careers during this period.

Beginning in 1947, the Toronto Maple Leafs, led by center Syl Apps, won the Stanley Cup three years in a row. In the early 1950s the Detroit Red Wings reigned supreme behind Gordie Howe and Terry Sawchuk. Montreal took over from there, thanks to players like Bernie "Boom Boom" Geoffrion, Dickie Moore, and Jacques Plante. In the 1960s, Bobby Hull

Shooting Stars

The first official NHL All-Star Game was played in 1947. Early on, the defending Stanley Cup champ would take on a collection of stars from the rest of the league. That format changed in 1966 when the NHL began to add new franchises. Today the league pits the Eastern Conference against the Western Conference.

The Toronto Maple Leafs celebrate their 1962 Stanley Cup championship, the first of three titles in a row.

and Bobby Orr revolutionized the game with their awesome speed and power.

The NHL's surge in popularity was accompanied by ice hockey's growth on American college campuses. The first official NCAA championship was held in 1948. Early on, the University of Michigan dominated the college tournament, but in time schools from the East evened the score.

Ice hockey also developed into a **compelling** Olympic event. Entering the 1960 Winter Games in Squaw Valley, California, Canada had won the gold medal every year except 1936. Then the U.S. squad shocked everyone on its home turf and won it all.

At the 1960 Winter Olympics, the United States used the home-ice advantage to break Canada's stranglehold on the gold medal.

Cracking the Color Line

The NHL's first black player was Willie O'Ree, who broke into the league with Boston in 1958. His career with the Bruins lasted only two years, although he continued to play in the minor leagues well into the 1970s.

It was almost a quarter-century before a black player made an impact in the NHL. This was partly because Canada produced most of the league's top stars, and the country's minority population was relatively small. But Grant Fuhr loved hockey as much as any Canadian kid. He became the goalie of the Edmonton Oilers in 1981, and helped the team to four Stanley Cups.

Fuhr inspired many young black players, including Jarome Iginla (#12, below). Though he started as a goalie, he shifted to the frontline, where he developed into the NHL's preeminent power forward. Iginla is part of a new generation of black players changing the face of hockey.

By now ice hockey looked very much like today's modern version. Players dressed in full protective gear, except for helmets. Goalies began to stray from their crease to handle the puck, and even wore masks.

Global Growth

In 1967, the NHL decided to capitalize on the game's increasing popularity. The league placed new teams in Los Angeles, Minnesota, Oakland, Philadelphia, Pittsburgh, and St. Louis. Over the next decade the NHL continued to expand. Players such as Guy Lafleur, Phil Esposito, Bobby Clarke, and Ken Dryden became superstars.

In 1972 the World Hockey Association began play. The rival league signed aging NHL stars to huge contracts, recruited gifted European players, and encouraged a wide-open, high-scoring style of play. Unfortunately, the sport was not ready for so many teams, and the WHA went out of business.

The NHL absorbed four WHA franchises in 1979, bringing its total number of teams to twenty-one. One of those was the Edmonton Oilers, which boasted a magnificent teenage center named Wayne Gretzky. Known as the "Great One," he shattered every major scoring record, and his popularity helped open the door to NHL expansion in warm-climate states like Florida and Texas. Ice hockey also got a boost when a team of U.S. amateurs stunned the powerful Soviet Union in

Ice Queens

Women's ice hockey has been part of Canadian culture for more than a century. The first game was held in Barrie, Ontario, in 1892. But the sport didn't catch on with American women until later. A Canadian named Manon Rheaume became a hero to women across North America when she appeared in a 1992 NHL pre-season game.

One woman who noticed Rheaume was Cammi Granato (above, on the left with team-mate Karen Bye). She had grown up in a family that loved ice hockey. Her brother, Tony, was an All-Star in the NHL. In 1998, she starred in the first women's Olympic ice hockey tournament and led Team USA to the gold medal. Now, girls all across the United States and Canada dream of being the next Cammi Granato or Manon Rheaume.

Many people consider Wayne Gretzky the greatest ice hockey player of all time.

the 1980 Olympics, and then went on to capture the gold medal.

Today, ice hockey is more popular than ever. In Canada it is considered the national **pastime**. In the United States, hundreds of thousands of boys and girls participate in programs sponsored by USA Hockey, the national organization that oversees the sport in the States. Fans visit the Hockey Hall of Fame and Museum in Toronto every year. The Olympic hockey tournament has become a highly anticipated event— especially now that pros are allowed to compete. NHL games, meanwhile, are televised nationally every week of the season. Rising stars like Paul Kariya, Jarome Iginla, and Joe Thornton are becoming household names, while also showing the league's increasing diversity.

Miracle Maker

The mastermind behind Team USA's 1980 "Miracle on Ice" was coach Herb Brooks. Ironically, he was the last player cut from the American team that had captured the gold in 1960.

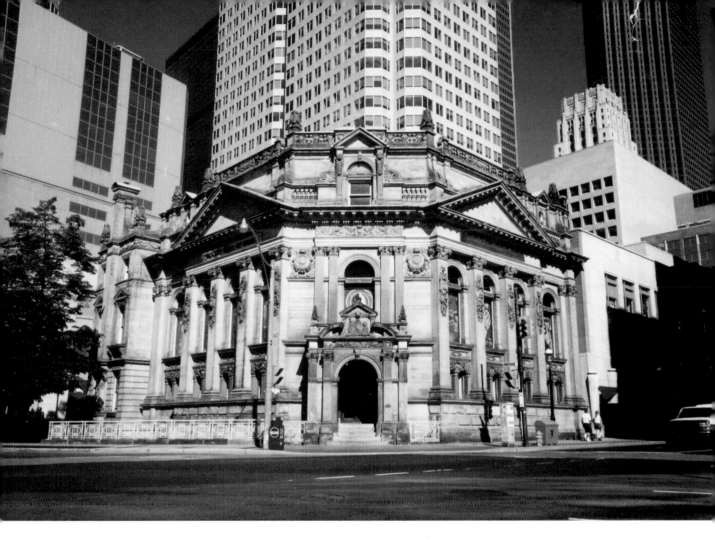

These are all incredible accomplishments given ice hockey's humble beginnings on the frozen ponds and rivers in the wilds of Canada. The best news is that the sport still has room to grow. In fact, many fans believe ice hockey's brightest days have yet to arrive.

The Hockey Hall of Fame and Museum is one of Toronto's more popular tourist attractions.

A goalie reaches high with his catching glove to snag a hard shot— What a save!

Chapter Two

Goal Oriented

The object of ice hockey is simple enough: put the puck in the net. But scoring a goal is easier said than done. Players must develop a variety of unrelated skills such as skating and stickhandling, then combine them on the ice. What's the best way to improve? Learn the fundamentals and practice them as much as possible.

Six Pack

Six players take the ice: center, two wings, two defensemen, and goalie. Only

Before a game starts, players on each team warm up by skating around the ice.

the goalie concentrates all his efforts on defense. The other five skaters must help out on both ends of the ice. Of course, the center and wings often think offense first, while the opposite is normally true of defensemen.

No one spends an entire game on the ice. Skating up and down the rink can be very tiring. Players take shifts that usually last about forty-five seconds to a minute. When not in the game, they sit on the bench with their teammates and wait for the coach to tell a new line of forwards or pair of defensemen to switch with the skaters on the ice. These changes can be made after play is stopped, or while players are speeding around the ice.

The center is looked upon as a playmaker. He is counted on to score goals and set up his teammates with good shots at the net. He often takes **face-offs** when he's on the ice. Speed, strong stickhandling skills, and good vision are very helpful at this position.

The right wing and left wing are often dangerous shooters. When on the attack, they are sometimes asked to dig along the boards to gain control of the puck. Other times they head for the front of the net and stay alert for rebounds. A good winger can either be a physical player who isn't afraid to use his body or a speedster who skates right by opponents.

Defensemen need good instincts and solid checking skills to break up plays in their end. Their first priority is to keep the puck away from their net. When they spot a scoring opportunity developing at the other end, they are encouraged to join the attack.

As the name suggests, the goalie is responsible for protecting the goal. He relies on good balance and quick feet and hands. **Lateral** movement and anticipation are essential, too. Netminders must be prepared to slide across the goalmouth and move out from the net to force opponents into more difficult shots. By thinking along with a shooter, a good goalie can make hard saves look relatively easy.

Quick Change Artists

When substitutions are made during live action it is called changing on the fly.

A goalie stretches to his right to try to block a shot.

Blocking a shot, however, is only half the job. Covering the puck and preventing rebounds is just as important. Lots of goals are scored when the puck squirts loose from a goalie and onto the stick of an opponent right in front of the net.

Skating and Checking

There's a common perception that strong skaters are born, not made. That's not true. Anyone can learn the proper way to skate and become very good at it.

In ice hockey different types of skating are needed in different situations. Free skating is all about moving straight ahead as fast as possible. Agility skating is crucial to changing direction and stopping and starting in a flash. A forward flying down the wing uses this skill to make a sharp cut toward the goal. Backward skating is particularly important to defensemen as the opponent approaches on an offensive rush.

Do these varied kinds of skating share anything in common? Yes. All require good balance and posture. Keep your feet a comfortable distance apart, and don't look down at your skates. Remember also to pump your arms the same way that sprinters and marathoners do when running. This helps generate speed and power.

Just like skating, there are many ways to check. In all cases, the object is to separate your opponent from the puck. The poke check, sweep check, and hook check are examples of the stick check. In each instance, the defender's stick never leaves

Geared Up

The rules of ice hockey stipulate that all players must wear proper protective gear. In youth leagues, this includes shin pads, shoulder pads, elbow pads, hip pads or padded hockey pants, gloves, a helmet with a face mask and chin strap, and a mouthpiece.

Goalies equip themselves with even more protection. They use thick leg pads that extend from the top of their skates to their thighs. The blocker, also known as the waffle because of its size and shape, is worn on the stick hand, and the catching glove goes on the other. The goalie mask covers the head entirely.

the ice. This makes it easier to knock the puck away from an opponent.

Smashing body checks, whether with the hip or shoulder, always draw oohs and aahs from fans. Aim for an opponent's

Hard body checks into the boards are allowed in the pros—and help make the NHL so exciting.

midsection, not his knees or head. Don't jump in the air when making a body check, or wrap your arms around the player.

Carrying, Passing, and Shooting

Shooting the puck requires much more than brute strength. Accuracy and control are equally if not more important. Good shooters can hit their target with amazing consistency.

When holding the stick, one hand goes at the top and the other slides about halfway down the **shaft**. If you're right-handed, your right hand should be lower on the stick. The opposite is true if you're a lefty.

The wrist shot whips the puck toward the net with surprising speed. It is executed with a smooth, quick turn of the wrists that sweeps the **stick blade** across the ice. This type of shot can also be performed on the backhand. The slap shot, by contrast, requires a much longer motion in which the stick swings like a pendulum. On the backswing and follow-through, the stick blade actually rises close to shoulder level.

Being able to carry the puck on your stick in the face of opposing pressure is an extremely valuable skill. There are three basic maneuvers: moving the puck side-to-side, diagonally, or front-to-back. Try to stickhandle with quick, short movements whenever possible. It's also important to keep your eyes focused on where you're going. As in all phases of ice hockey, the more in control you are, the better.

As this picture shows, good balance is required to shoot the puck with velocity and accuracy.

The ice surface is large and provides plenty of open space for every skater.

Chapter Three

Around the Rink

The size of an official NHL rink is 200 feet (61 meters) long and 85 feet (30 centimeters) wide. A wooden wall topped by see-through safety glass surrounds the ice surface. This partition is commonly known as the boards. Each of the rink's four corners is rounded to allow the puck to **careen** around the boards.

Getting in Line

The red center line divides the ice surface in half. There are two blue lines on either side of the red line. The area between the blue lines in the middle of the rink is called the neutral zone. The areas below the blue lines are known as either the attacking or defending zones.

Five circles are painted on the ice, one directly in the center and two in each end. This is where face-offs are held. They can also be held at any of the four dots just above the blue lines. The face-off circle at center ice is where players gather at the start of each period, and after a goal is scored. The other circles and dots may be used whenever an official whistles the play dead.

A goal—6 feet (1.8 m) wide and 4 feet (1.2 m) high—is placed at each end of the ice, several feet from the end boards.

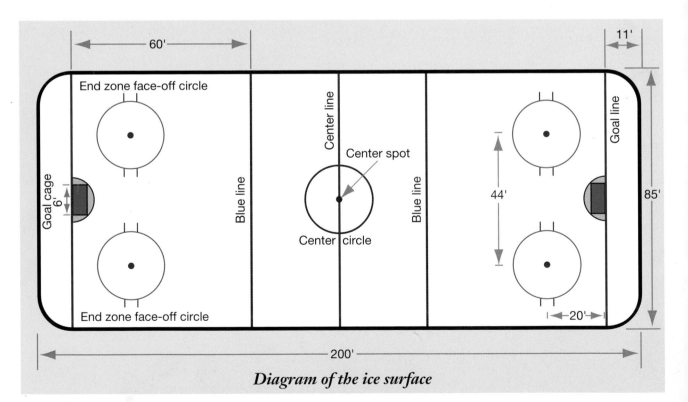

Diagram of the ice surface

Two posts connected by a crossbar along the top, all of which are made of metal, frame the goal. The net is fastened to the posts and crossbar. A red line known as the goal line runs across the bottom of the goal. The colored semicircle just in front of the net is the goal crease. No one is allowed to interfere with the goalie in this area.

Tied Up

NHL games are divided into three 20-minute periods. In youth leagues, the periods might not last as long. Players are given time to rest in the locker room between the first and second periods and between the second and third periods.

Interestingly, not all ice hockey games end with a winner and a loser. Sometimes a contest finishes in a tie. For example, if the score is knotted after time

As this picture shows, netminders have a lot of area to cover "between the pipes" of the goal.

At Long Last

The longest game in NHL history was a 1–0 playoff win by the Detroit Red Wings over the Montreal Maroons in 1936. It lasted 176 minutes and 30 seconds—or nearly nine periods! Mud Bruneteau broke the scoreless tie at 16:30 of the sixth overtime.

Seeing Red

There's no doubt when a goal is scored in the NHL. A red light behind the net flashes, and a loud siren blares throughout the arena.

Team Canada (above, in white) "lights the lamp" with a goal against Team USA during the 2002 Winter Olympics.

expires in the third period of an NHL regular-season game, the teams square off in a five-minute overtime period. The team that scores first wins. If neither team records a goal, the game is declared a tie. In the playoffs, there are no ties. Overtime periods run twenty minutes, and teams play on until someone scores a goal.

The way to win in ice hockey is to score more goals than your opponent. A goal is scored when the entire puck crosses the goal line. A shot that bangs off the post or crossbar and bounces away from the net is not a goal.

Boxed In

The referee and linesmen are responsible for enforcing the rules during an ice hockey game. They wear black-striped shirts, and skate around the ice watching the action very closely. The officials blow their whistles whenever they spot a violation of the rules.

In general, the referee looks for violent or dangerous plays. Using the stick in an unsafe manner almost always draws a whistle. Remember, a stick is not a weapon. Be careful on body checks, too. For example, don't drive a player into the boards from behind.

There is a long list of penalties that result in a visit to the penalty box. "Minor" infractions such as tripping, hooking, slashing, holding, elbowing, or roughing carry a two-minute

sentence. The penalized player cannot return to the ice until either his penalty time has expired or the team on the power play scores a goal. For major infractions like fighting, a player can be ejected from the game. These penalties also can land a player in the penalty box for a full five minutes, regardless of how many goals the opposition scores.

The linesmen concentrate on infractions that don't carry penalty time, but result in a face-off. For example, offsides is ruled when a player crosses the enemy blue line, and enters the attacking zone before the puck. Icing occurs when a player shoots the puck from his side of the center line across the opponent's red line (which extends from each side of the goal to the boards). If the team on defense (except for the goalie) touches the puck before the opposition, a face-off is held in the other team's end. Similar infractions include passing the puck across two lines and hitting the puck with a stick above the shoulders.

One-Up, One-Down

There's no worse place to be during an ice hockey game than in the penalty box. When a player is in the box, his team has one less player on the ice, which makes defending the goal much more difficult.

Duties change when a player is sent to the penalty box. The team with the extra skater is on the power play. The forwards try to control the puck in the attacking zone, while the defensemen position themselves just inside the opponent's blue line on the "point." The object is to pass the puck around quickly to create open shots at the net.

Everyone on the shorthanded team, meanwhile, works to clear the puck from their zone. Forwards and defensemen avoid taking risks. Their job is to kill time, and keep the opponent under wraps until the teams return to even strength.

Mark Messier combined speed, power, and on-ice artistry to become one of hockey's all-time greats.

Chapter Four

Fast and Furious

Throughout ice hockey's evolution, a tug of war has waged between two styles of play. Some believe the game's essence is fast skating and precision passing in open ice. Others feel that the sport owes its heritage to a tough, blue-collar work ethic. Is speed king, or does might make right?

East vs. West

In many ways, the debate between speed and power boils down to a face-off between North American hockey and

European hockey. Though Canada prides itself on being the sport's nerve center, many countries have played just as long, including those across the Atlantic Ocean. There, ice hockey evolved a bit differently. Greater emphasis was placed on stickhandling, passing, and skating.

European rinks and rules reflect this difference in philosophy. Ice surfaces are larger, giving players more room to maneuver. The rules promote an open style of play. For example, passes across two lines are legal. This encourages players

In the style of play that developed in North America, hard hits have always been part of the game.

to spread out over the ice, and look for opportunities to sneak behind the defense.

For a long time North Americans, especially Canadians, were unimpressed by European ice hockey. It's not that they frowned upon fancy passing plays and swift skating. But they believed physical **intimidation** was part of the game, too. In the smaller rinks of Canada and the United States, bone-crunching collisions were a risk players were willing to take. Indeed, they often paid with their bodies when trying to score a goal. And if sometimes two opponents dropped their gloves and threw punches, so be it.

Playing Catch Up

For nearly fifty years, the North American style of ice hockey proved superior in international competition. Canada won gold in six of the first seven Olympics. The United States finished second on four of those occasions.

The International Ice Hockey Federation hosted the first World Championship in 1910. Canada dominated that

After the 1972 Summit Series, players from Canada and the Soviet Union gained newfound respect for each other.

tournament, too. By the 1950s, however, the rest of the world began to catch up. The Soviet Union led the way, developing an **intricate** system in which forwards and defensemen were grouped together in units of five. Czechoslovakia, Finland, and Sweden also took their games to new heights.

In 1972, Canada and the Soviet Union squared off in an eight-game Summit Series to determine which hockey superpower was tops. Because North America and the USSR were sworn enemies at the time, there was a great deal riding on the outcome. Canada's squad included all-time greats such as Bobby Orr, Phil Esposito, and Frank Mahovlich. The Soviets countered with Valeri Kharlamov, Alexander Yakushev, and Boris Mikhalov. Though the Canadians claimed a dramatic victory in the final game, the real winner was the game of ice hockey. Suddenly the sport was open to exciting new possibilities.

Mixing and Matching

The impact of the Summit Series was felt throughout the ice hockey world. For years it was assumed that European players weren't tough enough to hack it in the hard-knocks world of the NHL. Now the league grudgingly admitted that it might be wrong.

Some of Europe's top stars got their feet wet in the WHA. Others went directly to the NHL. Börje Salming, Anders Hedberg, and Ulf Nilsson led the first generation of talented foreign players to make it big in North America. The next round came along in the 1980s, and included the Stastny brothers (Anton, Marian, and Peter), Jari Kurri, and Kent Nilsson.

International Appeal

The 1972 Summit Series spawned many new international tournaments. The Canada Cup debuted in 1976, and quickly became the sport's most prized international trophy. It has since been renamed the World Cup of Hockey.

The World Junior Championship (for players under the age of twenty) was first held in 1977.

Today the tournament is a must-see event for pro scouts searching for future NHL stars. The picture above shows action from the 2003 World Junior Championship.

The Women's World Championship premiered in 1990. Canada won the first five competitions before the United States captured the crown in 2001.

Canada's two greatest players ever—Wayne Gretzky and Mario Lemieux—also established their legends in the 1980s. Significantly, they did so playing a European style. Meanwhile, players born outside North America, such as Peter Forsberg and Jaromir Jagr, found that adding a little muscle to their games made them more effective.

Today's emerging stars can't be placed in a single category. Tough players such as Chris Drury and Jarome Iginla are also wonderful skaters, passers, and stickhandlers. Indeed, it seems that they have settled the argument between speed and power by relying on generous portions of both.

Mario Lemieux, nicknamed "Super Mario," is one of the greatest scorers in NHL history.

Dany Heatley, who won the 2002 Calder Trophy, also took home the MVP trophy after the 2003 NHL All-Star Game.

Chapter Five

Power Players

Choosing ice hockey's all-time best players isn't easy. A player's era, the innovations he brought to the game, and the number of championships he won all figure into the debate.

Goalies

In Georges Vezina's era, netminders weren't allowed to drop to the ice to make a save. His ability to stay cool under fire made him the best in the business. From 1910 to 1926, he won two

NHA titles and two Stanley Cups. The trophy given annually to the NHL's top goalie is named after him.

Bill Durnan deserved a hand every time he took the ice. Make that two. Durnan was ambidextrous, and used special gloves that allowed him to hold the stick in either hand. From 1943 to 1950, he collected six Vezina trophies.

Three goalies set the pace in the 1950s and 1960s. Cat-quick and wonderfully instinctive, Terry Sawchuk was a shooter's worst nightmare. During his twenty-year career he captured four Stanley Cups, and set NHL records for wins (447) and shutouts (103).

Jacques Plante, the first goalie to wear a mask, earned the Vezina Trophy seven times. He hated the thought of surrendering a goal, especially in the playoffs. During his career, he

During his Hall of Fame career, Patrick Roy was at his best when his team needed him the most.

posted a 2.17 goals against average in the post-season, and won six Stanley Cups.

Glenn Hall's mastery in the net was matched by his durability. He was the first goalie to drop to his knees and flare his skates out to the sides to protect the bottom of the net. From 1955 to 1962 Hall started and finished 502 games in a row.

In the present era, Patrick Roy and Dominik Hasek are the top goalies. Roy ranks as perhaps the best clutch netminder in NHL history. Hasek, one of the most unorthodox goalies ever, was so hard to score on because shooters never knew what to expect from him.

Smart Move

Ken Dryden's best piece of equipment was his mind. Dryden left nothing to chance, preparing for each game by studying his opponent's strengths and weaknesses. During the 1970s, he won six Stanley Cups with Montreal.

Defensemen

There has never been a tougher player than Eddie Shore. From 1926 to 1940, the hard-hitting defenseman broke his jaw five times and his nose fourteen times, and required 973 stitches to sew up a wide assortment of cuts. He won the Hart Trophy as the NHL's MVP four times.

Two defensemen who entered the league in the 1940s made lasting impressions. Though Red Kelly was a dangerous offensive threat along the blue line, his defensive presence set him apart. Kelly played on eight Stanley Cup champs.

Before Doug Harvey came along, teams often dropped two forwards back to help on defense. But Harvey was so skilled at stealing the puck and triggering an offensive rush with an outlet pass that his teams didn't need back-checkers. Honored seven times with the Norris Trophy as the NHL's best defenseman, he captured six Stanley Cups.

Bobby Orr, who combined defensive smarts with the skills of a high-scoring forward, was the first defenseman to tally 100 points in a season. The winner of the Norris Trophy each year from 1968 to 1975, Orr was voted league MVP three times, and twice earned the Ross Trophy.

In 1970, Bobby Orr (#4) clinched the Stanley Cup for the Boston Bruins with this amazing high-flying goal.

In the 1970s and 1980s, Denis Potvin followed in Orr's footsteps, while Larry Robinson and Rob Langway put the "defense" back in defenseman. Then came Ray Borque, Paul Coffey, and Chris Chelios. They are the cream of the crop of ice hockey's most recent generation of All-Star defenders.

Forward

The first group of players who specialized in putting the puck in the net hit the scene in the early 1900s. Fred "Cyclone" Taylor skated faster backward than most players did forward. "Phantom" Joe Malone was a lethal scorer who set the stage for modern centers. His linemate, Newsy Lalonde, had few peers as a playmaker.

Howie Morenz was known as the Babe Ruth of Canada. The NHL's preeminent star in the 1920s and 1930s, he could do it all on the ice. Away from the rink, no player was more beloved by the fans.

Syl Apps gave Morenz a run for his money in the 1940s. In leading the Toronto Maple Leafs to three Stanley Cups, he became a hero to hockey fans everywhere. The **consummate** gentleman, Apps picked up just 56 minutes in penalties during his ten-year career.

Maurice Richard may have been the toughest competitor ever to lace up a pair of skates. Nicknamed the "Rocket" for his explosive speed and hot temper, he was the first NHL player to score 50 goals in a season and 500 in a career. From 1942 to 1960, he led Montreal to eight Stanley Cups.

As Richard's career was winding down, Jean Beliveau took over as Montreal's on-ice leader. Beliveau inspired a generation of young players with his refined style and intelligent play.

Gordie Howe is known as "Mr. Hockey." A rookie in 1946, he played professionally until his fifty-second birthday thirty-four years later. Second on the NHL's all-time scoring list, Howe was as feisty as he was talented. Opponents feared his elbows as much as they feared his shot.

Bobby Hull may have been the fastest skating forward in history, and his slapshot was once clocked at 118 mph. The "Golden Jet" was the first to score 50 goals in a season more than once. Hull roamed freely on the ice partly because of his teammate, Stan Mikita. He started his career in 1959 as Hull's "bodyguard," but soon abandoned his brutish ways and retired as one of the game's most admired players.

Bobby Hull was known as the "Golden Jet" because of his blonde hair and incredible speed. His son, Brett, also became an NHL star.

In the 1970s Guy Lafleur electrified fans with his **free-wheeling** style of play. During his prime, no player was more exciting to watch.

Bobby Clarke went about things a bit differently. He was tenacious, talented, and afraid of nobody.

Wayne Gretzky ushered the game into the current era. The "Great One" broke every offensive record during his twenty-year career. Along the way he was voted league MVP nine times and won four Stanley Cups.

Had Mario Lemieux not battled cancer and a painful back injury, he might have surpassed Gretzky's records. When healthy, "Super Mario" was unstoppable. From 1984 to 1997 he averaged more than two points per game.

Is the next Gretzky, Lemieux, Orr, or Roy just discovering ice hockey in a youth league or on a frozen pond somewhere? Perhaps. Or maybe there's a boy or girl right now who's learning to combine his or her skills in a way no one has ever imagined. Creativity and hard work have always been the keys to success in ice hockey. If you let your imagination run wild and give it your best shot, that next superstar could turn out to be you.

Ice hockey is an exciting sport—for fans of every age and players of every skill level.

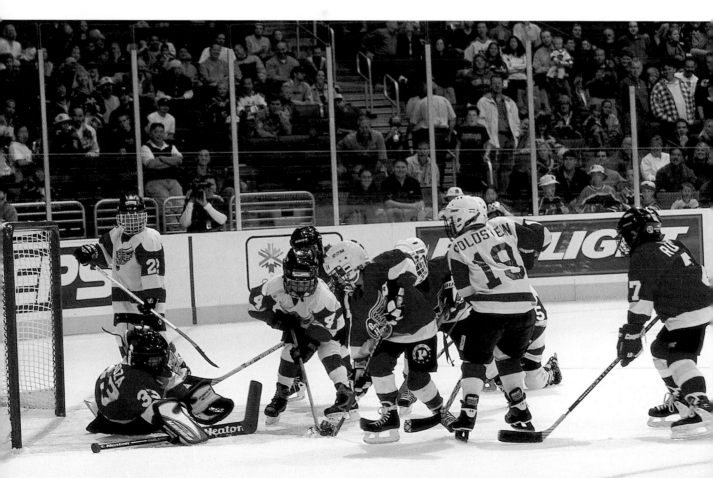

Timeline

1885	The first ice hockey league is formed in Kingston, Ontario.
1893	The Montreal AAAs become the first team to win the Stanley Cup.
1904	John "Doc" Gibson starts the International Pro Hockey League in Michigan.
1905	Frank McGee of the Ottawa Silver scores 14 goals in on Stanley Cup game.
1909	The National Hockey Association begins play.
1911	The NHA settles on six skaters per side.
1912	The Pacific Coast Hockey Association forms.
1917	The NHA suspends play, and is reorganized into the National Hockey League.
1923	An NHL game is broadcast on the radio for the first time.
1924	Canada wins the first Olympic gold medal in ice hockey.
1929	The NHL allows forward passing in the attacking zone.
1934	An NHL All-Star game is organized as a benefit for injured star Ace Bailey.
1938	The Chicago Blackhawks, whose roster includes eight American-born players, capture the Stanley Cup.
1943	After NHL president Frank Calder dies, the league introduces the Calder Cup, the trophy awarded to the rookie of the year.
1944	Maurice Richard becomes the first NHL player to score 50 goals in one season.
1948	Michigan wins the first NCAA ice hockey championship.
1954	The Norris Trophy, awarded to the NHL's top defenseman, is introduced.
1958	Willie O'Ree breaks the NHL's color barrier.

1960	The U.S. wins the ice hockey gold medal at the Winter Games in Squaw Valley, California.
1965	Jean Beliveau of Montreal earns the first Conn Smythe Trophy, awarded to the most outstanding player in the postseason.
1967	The NHL adds the California Seals, Los Angeles Kings, Minnesota North Stars, Pittsburgh Penguins, and St. Louis Blues.
1969	Phil Esposito of Boston becomes the first player to top 100 points in an NHL season.
1970	Bobby Orr of Boston becomes the first defenseman to top 100 points in an NHL season.
1972	Canada defeats the Soviet Union in the Summit Series.
1973	The Hartford Whalers win the first World Hockey Association championship.
1979	The WHA plays its final season, and seventeen-year-old Wayne Gretzky finishes third in the league in scoring.
1980	The U.S. shocks the world by winning the ice hockey gold medal at the Olympics in Lake Placid, New York.
1982	Wayne Gretzky becomes the first player to top 200 points in an NHL season.
1988	Mario Lemieux dethrones Gretzky as the NHL scoring champ.
1993	The Anaheim Ducks and Florida Panthers join the NHL.
1998	NHL players are allowed to compete in the Olympics for the first time, and the U.S. wins the first women's ice hockey tournament at the Winter Games.
2001	In his twenty-first and final season, Ray Borque leads the Colorado Avalanche to the Stanley Cup.
2002	Canada and the U.S. square off in the men's and women's ice hockey gold medal games at the Olympics. The Canadians win both.

Glossary

ardent—showing great enthusiasm

careen—to move forward at a high speed

compelling—attracting strong interest

consummate—excellent or skillful

controversial—causing strong disagreement

demise—to die slowly

face-off—a hockey term describing when two opponents battle for control of a puck dropped by the referee after a stoppage in play

freewheeling—to move about without boundaries or restrictions

goal crease—the area in front of the net where it is illegal to interfere with the goalie

intimidation—persuading someone to do something through threats

intricate—complicated or sophisticated

lateral—side-to-side movement

pastime—a hobby, interest, or activity

shaft—the straight part of the stick that extends up from the blade

stick blade—the flat, bottom part of the stick used to control the puck

stickhandle—to control the puck with a hockey stick

teetering—to be in the position where things can go wrong

To Find Out More

Books

Diamond, Dan (editor). *Total Hockey*. New York, NY: Total Sports, 1998. (Updated periodically)

Duplacey, James & Zweig, Eric. *A Century of Hockey Heroes*. New York, NY: Somerville House Books Limited & NHL Enterprises, L.P., 1999.

Stewart, Mark. *Hockey: A History of the Fastest Game on Ice*. Danbury, CT: Franklin Watts, 1998.

Stewart, Mark. *The Stanley Cup*. Danbury, CT: Franklin Watts, 2003.

Any of the hockey biographies in the New Wave series by Mark Stewart published by the Millbrook Press.

Organizations and Online Sites

http://www.ncaachampionships.com
Official site of all NCAA championships, including ice hockey's "Frozen Four."

http:// www.whockey.com
A fan site devoted to women's ice hockey, including news on camps and tournaments.

Hockey Hall of Fame
http://www.hhof.com/
Official site of the Hockey Hall of Fame. Learn about all of the hall's members through detailed biographies and statistics, and get a 3-D look at the Stanley Cup.

National Hockey League
http://www.nhl.com
Official site of the National Hockey League. Read about your favorite players, and follow links to your favorite teams.

USA Hockey
http://www.usahockey.com
Official site of USA Hockey. Keep tabs on the national teams that represent the United States in international competition, including player profiles and statistics.

A Note on Sources

In researching this book, I tried to reference as many sources as possible. I consulted another author named Mark Stewart, who has written books on hockey, including biographies of famous players. I also went to my local library and checked out a wide variety of books. Web sites on the Internet, including the one hosted by the National Hockey League, were helpful as well.

—Mike Kennedy

Index

Numbers in *italics* indicate illustrations.

About the Author

From Ichiro to the Indy 500 and the Super Bowl to skateboarding, Mike Kennedy has covered it all in the world of sports. A graduate of Franklin & Marshall College, he has profiled athletes such as Sammy Sosa, Tony Hawk, and Venus and Serena Williams. Mike has contributed his expertise to other books by Grolier/Scholastic, including *The World Series*, *The Super Bowl*, and *The NBA Finals*. He is also a co-creator of JockBio.com (*www.jock bio.com*), a unique website that profiles popular sports personalities.

His other titles in this series are *Baseball*, *Football*, *Basketball*, *Roller Hockey*, *Skateboarding*, and *Soccer*.